INVESTIGATION REPORT

METHANOL TANK EXPLOSION AND FIRE

(2 Dead, 1 Critically Injured)

I0488881

BETHUNE POINT WASTEWATER TREATMENT PLANT

CITY OF DAYTONA BEACH, FLORIDA

JANUARY 11, 2006

KEY ISSUES:

- HAZARD COMMUNICATION

- HOT WORK CONTROL

- PLASTIC PIPE IN FLAMMABLE SERVICE

- FLAME ARRESTER MAINTENANCE

- FLORIDA PUBLIC EMPLOYEE SAFETY PROGRAMS

REPORT NO. 2006-03-I-FL

MARCH 2007

Contents

Figures

Tables

Acronyms and Abbreviations

ASME	American Society of Mechanical Engineers
BNR	Biological Nutrient Removal
BOCA	Building Officials Code Administrators
CDM	Camp Dresser & McKee Inc.
CFR	Code of Federal Regulations
CSB	U. S. Chemical Safety and Hazard Investigation Board
FAC	Florida Administrative Code
HAZCOM	Hazard Communication
IRIC	Indian River Industrial Contractors
MSDS	Material Safety Data Sheet
NACE	National Association of Corrosion Engineers
NFPA	National Fire Protection Association
NPS	Nominal Pipe Size
OJT	On-the-Job Training
OSHA	Occupational Safety and Health Administration
pH	Hydrogen Ion Concentration
PVC	Polyvinyl Chloride
SCBA	Self Contained Breathing Apparatus
WEF	Water Environment Federation
WWTP	Wastewater Treatment Plant

Executive Summary

On January 11, 2006, an explosion and fire occurred at the City of Daytona Beach, Bethune Point Wastewater Treatment Plant (Bethune Point WWTP) in Daytona Beach, Florida, killing two employees and severely burning a third.

The Bethune Point WWTP processes wastewater using a treatment that requires the addition of methanol, a highly flammable liquid. The methanol is stored in an aboveground storage tank.

The U.S. Chemical Safety and Hazard Investigation Board (CSB) determined that maintenance workers using a cutting torch on a roof above the methanol storage tank accidentally ignited vapors coming from the tank vent. The flame flashed back into the storage tank, causing an explosion inside the tank that precipitated multiple methanol piping failures and a large fire that engulfed the tank and workers.

The investigation identified the following root causes:

The City of Daytona Beach

- did not implement adequate controls for hot work at the Bethune Point WWTP, and

- had a hazard communication program that did not effectively communicate the hazards associated with methanol at the Bethune Point WWTP.

The investigation identified the following contributing causes:

- The City of Daytona Beach has no program to evaluate the safety of non-routine tasks.

- The piping and valves in the methanol system were constructed of polyvinyl chloride in lieu of steel.

- An aluminum flame arrester was installed on the methanol tank vent even though methanol corrodes aluminum.

- The operation and maintenance manual for the Bethune Point WWTP did not include a requirement to maintain the flame arrester.

This CSB report makes recommendations to the Governor and Legislature of the State of Florida; the City of Daytona Beach; the U.S. Department of Labor, Occupational Safety and Health Administration; the National Fire Protection Association; the Water Environment Federation; the Methanol Institute; and Camp Dresser & McKee Inc.

1.0 INTRODUCTION

1.1 Background

On January 11, 2006, an explosion and fire occurred at the City of Daytona Beach, Bethune Point WWTP in Daytona Beach, Florida. Two employees died and one was severely burned after a worker using a cutting torch accidentally ignited vapors coming from the methanol storage tank vent. An explosion inside the tank followed, causing the attached piping to fail and release about 3,000 gallons of methanol, which burned.

1.2 Investigative Process

Investigators from the U.S. Chemical Safety and Hazard Investigation Board (CSB) arrived at the facility on January 13, 2006. The CSB examined and collected physical evidence from the incident, interviewed Bethune WWTP employees and others, and reviewed relevant documents. The CSB coordinated its work with a number of other investigative organizations, including:

- Division of the State Fire Marshal, State of Florida;

- City of Daytona Beach Police Department; and

- City of Daytona Beach Fire Department.

1.3 City of Daytona Beach

The City of Daytona Beach, located on the east coast of central Florida in Volusia County, has about 64,000 residents and is governed by a city commission composed of a mayor and six elected commissioners. The commission hires a city manager who presents a budget for the commission's approval, oversees city operations, and manages about 800 city employees.

The Bethune Point WWTP is part of the Waste/Water group in the Utilities department, whose director reports to the city manager.

1.4   Bethune Wastewater Treatment Plant

Eleven city employees operate the Bethune Point WWTP, treating about 13 million gallons per day before discharging to the Halifax River (Figure 1).

Figure 1. Bethune Point WWTP.
(Picture courtesy of the City of Daytona Beach)

The plant originally used conventional wastewater treatment. This treatment is appropriate for the wastewater that Bethune Point receives, but is ineffective at removing nitrogen and phosphorus compounds that promote algae growth.

In the late 1980s, the State of Florida required wastewater treatment plants to reduce the discharge of compounds that promote algae growth. The City of Daytona Beach contracted Camp Dresser & McKee Inc.[1] (CDM) in 1989 to redesign the Bethune Point plant to incorporate an advanced wastewater treatment process to remove nitrogen and phosphorus compounds. CDM's scope of work was to specify the process, develop the conceptual and detailed designs, prepare construction and project specifications, and oversee construction. The City of Daytona Beach separately contracted Indian River Industrial Contractors (IRIC) to build the advanced wastewater treatment process. Operation of the new process started in 1993.

1.5   Advanced Wastewater Treatment Process

Advanced wastewater treatment is a biological nutrient removal (BNR) process where specialized bacteria, with the addition of an organic nutrient, convert nitrogen compounds into nitrogen gas. The Bethune Point WWTP uses methanol as the organic nutrient for the bacteria. Chemical metering pumps continuously fed methanol to the process from a 10,000-gallon carbon steel storage tank.

In 1999, the City of Daytona Beach modified the BNR process to operate without the continuous methanol feed; however, the facility continued to use the methanol system and 10,000-gallon storage tank for sporadic methanol addition. As a result, the facility maintained a large inventory of methanol even though demand was substantially reduced. The methanol storage tank contained between 2,000 and 3,000 gallons when the incident occurred.

_____

[1] CDM is a multinational consulting, engineering, and construction firm specializing in water and wastewater treatment facilities.

1.6 Methanol

Methanol (commonly known as methyl or wood alcohol) is a Class 1B flammable liquid with a flash point of 54°F (12°C); its explosive limits are 6 to 36.5 volume percent in air. Methanol vapors are heavier than air with a vapor density (air=1) of 1.1.[2]

Methanol vapors burn with a colorless flame in daylight, although the presence of other materials can color the flame. Methanol is a skin and eye irritant and highly toxic when ingested.[3]

In addition to wastewater treatment, methanol is used in the manufacture of numerous consumer products including plastics, paints, adhesives, and fuels.[4]

The Methanol Institute represents manufacturers of methanol and distributes health, safety, and environmental information on the use and distribution of methanol.

1.7 Water Environment Federation

The Water Environment Federation (WEF) is a not-for-profit technical and educational organization with members from the wastewater industry. WEF offers training programs, workshops, and seminars. In addition, WEF publishes technical manuals and other information for the wastewater industry.

_____

[2] Lewis, R., 2000. *Sax's Dangerous Properties of Industrial Materials* (10th Edition).

[3] Ibid.

[4] Methanol Institute website, 2006, www.methanol.org.

2.0   Incident Description

2.1   Pre-Incident Events

In 2004 and 2005, several hurricanes damaged the Bethune Point WWTP, including two metal roofs used to shade two chemical storage areas. Facility personnel removed one of the damaged metal roofs in 2005 without incident. The second metal roof, installed over the methanol storage tank, was about 30 feet above the ground and more difficult to access. In consultation with the facility superintendent, the lead mechanic determined that facility personnel could remove the second damaged metal roof using a city-owned crane and a rented man-lift. The lead mechanic planned the job to remove the metal roof. The facility superintendent did not review details of the job and possible hazards.

On Monday, January 9, 2006, the lead mechanic and a mechanic prepared to remove the metal roof. They retrieved the man-lift and crane from other city facilities. The lead mechanic then familiarized himself with the operation of the man-lift. Workers at the Bethune Point WWTP had previously used the city crane and were familiar with its operation.

On Tuesday, January 10, 2006, the lead mechanic, the mechanic, and a third worker began removing the metal roof over the methanol storage tank. Standing in the man-lift, the lead mechanic and mechanic cut the metal roof into sections with an oxy-acetylene cutting torch and attached the cut sections to the crane hook. The third worker operated the crane to lower the cut sections to the ground. While cutting the metal roof, sparks from the torch ignited a grass fire. The crane operator extinguished the grass fire with a garden hose. In the early afternoon, the workers ran out of oxygen for the cutting torch and stopped work for the day. The lead mechanic ordered another oxygen cylinder so the job could resume on Wednesday.

2.2   The Incident

On Wednesday, January 11, 2006, three workers[5] continued the roof removal. About 11:15 a.m., the lead mechanic and the third worker were cutting the metal roof directly above the methanol tank vent. Sparks, showering down from the cutting torch, ignited methanol vapors coming from the vent, creating a fireball on top of the tank. The fire flashed through a flame arrester on the vent, igniting methanol vapors and air inside the tank, causing a explosion inside the steel tank. Figure 2 is an overview of the accident site showing the crane, man-lift, and tank after the incident.

Figure 2. Bethune Point WWTP accident site.

(Picture courtesy of the City of Daytona Beach)

---

[5] The workers included the lead mechanic and mechanic who worked on January 9 and 10, 2006 and a new worker from the facility.

The explosion inside the methanol storage tank

- rounded the tank's flat bottom, permanently deforming the tank and raising the side wall about one foot;

- ripped the nuts from six bolts used to anchor the tank to a concrete foundation;

- blew the flame arrester off the tank vent pipe;

- blew a level sensor off a 4-inch flange on the tank top;

- separated two 1-inch pipes, valves, and an attached level switch from flanges on the side of the tank;

- separated a 4-inch tank outlet pipe from the tank outlet valve; and

- separated a 4-inch tank fill pipe near the top the tank.

Methanol discharged from the separated pipes ignited and burned, spreading the fire. Methanol also flowed into the containment around the tank and through a drain to the WWTP where it was diluted and harmlessly processed.

The lead mechanic and the third worker were in the man-lift basket over the methanol tank when the ignition occurred. They were likely burned from the initial fireball and burning methanol vapors discharging from the tank vent under pressure from the explosion. The lead mechanic, fully engulfed in fire, likely jumped or fell from the man-lift. Emergency responders found his body within the concrete containment next to the tank.

The third worker stated that he had been partially out of the man-lift basket leaning over the roof when the fire ignited. On fire, he climbed onto the roof to escape. Co-workers, unable to reach him with a ladder, told him to jump to an adjacent lower roof and then to the ground. He sustained second and third-degree burns over most of his body, and was hospitalized for 4 months before being released to a medical rehabilitation facility.

Methanol sprayed from separated pipes onto the crane, burning the crane cab with the mechanic inside. On fire, he exited the cab and was assisted by co-workers. He died in the hospital the following day.

2.3   Emergency Response

Bethune Point WWTP workers heard the explosion and immediately went to the scene of the fire and aided the victims. The facility superintendent and a facility operator called 911 to report the incident and request fire and medical assistance. City Fire Station # 1 dispatched the first unit at 11:18 a.m., which arrived at Bethune Point WWTP at 11:22 a.m. When the unit arrived, the methanol and an adjacent empty tank were fully involved in the fire.

Firefighters provided first aid to the two burn victims and set up a fire monitor to provide a continuous stream of water onto burning insulation on the adjacent tank. Firefighters then evacuated everyone to an assembly point outside the main gate. The Volusia County Hazardous Materials (HAZMAT) Team also responded and assumed control of the firefighting effort. Firefighters extinguished the fire later that afternoon. The HAZMAT Team emergency responders recovered the body of the first victim the following day.

In addition to the three victims of the fire, 14 people sought medical evaluation. They included nine firefighters, four Bethune Point WWTP employees, and one police officer. After evaluation, one firefighter was transported to the hospital, treated, and released. There were no off-site consequences from this incident.

3.0 Analysis

The following sections analyze several causes CSB identified (Appendix A) including

- a lack of methanol hazard recognition;

- a lack of safety and hazard review in job planning;

- methanol piping failure; and

- an ineffective flame arrester.

3.1 Chemical Hazard Recognition

Chemical hazard recognition is commonly addressed through a hazard communication (HAZCOM) program that provides employees with information on chemical hazards and trains them on specific hazards and the use of available information. OSHA standards[6] require HAZCOM programs, however the City of Daytona Beach is not required to comply with these standards (Section 4.0). Although not required by regulation, the City of Daytona Beach maintains and makes available written information on chemical hazards and conducts safety and HAZCOM training.

As part of the investigation, the CSB analyzed Bethune Point WWTP employee continuing training records for safety and HAZCOM for 12 years preceding the incident; Table 1 lists these safety training topics. Of these, the City offered HAZCOM (also known as Right-to-Know) training only seven times and not since 2002. OSHA standards require employers to conduct HAZCOM training annually.

---

[6] 29 CFR Part 1910, Occupational Safety and Health Standards.

Table 1. Bethune Point WWTP safety training classes from 1994-2005.

Safety Training Topic	Sessions Conducted	Last Year Conducted
Gas Detector	2	2005
Lockout Tagout	3	2004
Self Contained Breathing Apparatus (SCBA)	11	2003
Fire Extinguisher	1	2003
Confined Space	2	2002
Right-to-Know – Material Safety Data Sheets (HAZCOM)	7	2002
Heat Exhaustion - Hot Environment	3	2001
Blood Borne Pathogens	2	2000
Fall Arrester	2	2000
Ultra Violet Lamps	1	2000
Uninterruptible Power Supply	1	2000
Air Pac (SCBA)	6	1999
Process Hazard Analysis Team Meeting	1	1998
Vehicular safety	1	1997
Fire Safety	1	1997
Foot Protection Awareness	1	1997
Entry Retrieval System	1	1996
Back Safety	1	1995

The city used a variety of training resources, including the Daytona Beach Fire Department; private contractors; equipment suppliers; and city personnel.

The contract for the 1993 plant upgrade that added the methanol system included a requirement for staff training; however, a detailed record of this training was unavailable. While a training abstract found in the contract files listed training topics, the CSB could not determine from this abstract if the methanol storage tank, flame arrester, and methanol hazards were covered. Interviewed employees remembered some methanol system training in 1993, but none could identify the purpose of the flame arrester or how the tank vented. In addition, employees could not remember if any of the HAZCOM (Right-to-Know)

training sessions covered methanol hazards.

Up to calendar year 2000, the City offered an average of five safety-related training sessions at Bethune

Point WWTP each year; however, since 2000 the number of such sessions[7] declined steadily (Figure 3).

This decline may have been influenced by the repeal of the Florida public employee safety law (2000)

and the elimination of City of Daytona Beach full-time Safety Position (2004).

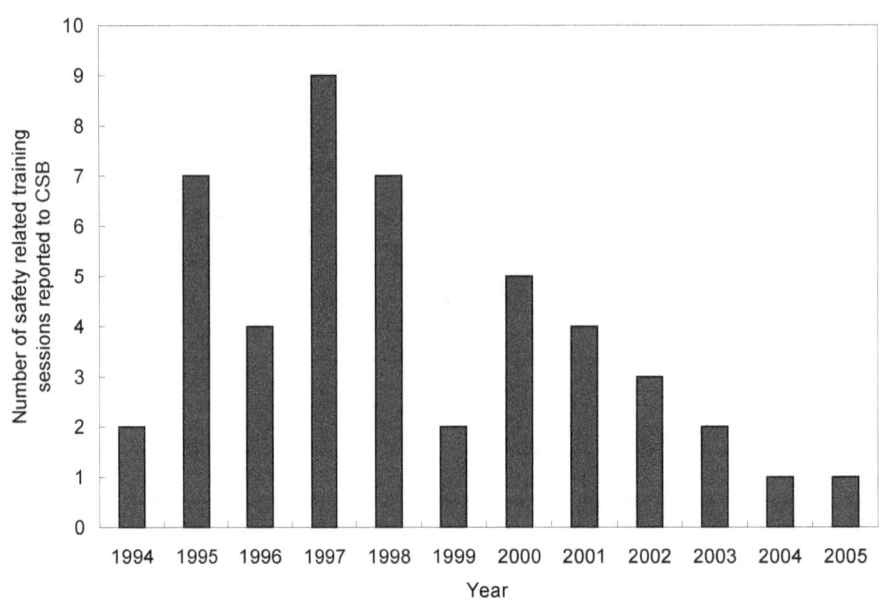

Figure 3. Bethune Point WWTP safety related training sessions.

In summary, the CSB found that the scope, content, and frequency of the HAZCOM training provided to

Bethune Point WWTP employees did not adequately prepare them to deal with the hazards associated

with flammable materials such as methanol.

---

[7] Many of the sessions were less than 1 hour in length.

3.2   Safety and Hazard Review in Job Planning

The CSB found that the City of Daytona Beach had not implemented a systematic method for identifying

hazards during non-routine work,[8] nor did the City have a permit-to-work system. Non-routine tasks can

be among the most hazardous at any facility. The lack of formal written procedures and general

unfamiliarity with the work increase the risk of these tasks. A permit-to-work system is a widely used

technique for evaluating hazards of non-routine work. Had the city used a permit-to-work system or other

work control practice, this incident may have been prevented.

The objective of permit-to-work systems is to ensure that non-routine work is properly planned and

authorized prior to commencing. Generally, a designated individual who is not the planner or executor of

the work signs the permit authorizing the work to proceed. This individual is typically a supervisor,

safety technician, or senior operator.

Permits can be issued to control any type of work, but those that are inherently hazardous are the most

important. Lees (2001) and the Center for Chemical Process Safety (CCPS) (1995) list hazardous

activities, including hot work[9], that especially warrant inclusion in a permit system

---

[8] Examples of non-routine work can include repairs, corrective maintenance, troubleshooting, and infrequent tasks.

[9] Hot work is defined as any work that may be a source of ignition, including open flames, cutting and welding, sparking of electrical equipment, grinding, buffing, drilling, chipping, sawing, or other similar operations that create hot metal sparks or hot surfaces from friction or impact.

3.3   Methanol Piping

3.3.1   Piping Design

CDM, the methanol system designer, specified[10] polyvinyl chloride (PVC) piping, valves, and fittings for all of the above- and below ground piping in the methanol system.

The aboveground PVC piping (Figure 4) included:

- a 4-inch nominal pipe size (NPS) fill pipe that connected a flange on the top of the tank to a fill connection near ground level;

- a 4-inch NPS outlet pipe, connected to a valve on a flange near the bottom of the tank that supplied the methanol pumps;

- two 1-inch NPS pipes and PVC valves that connected a level switch to two flanges near the bottom of the tank; and

- a 4-inch NPS vent pipe connected to a flange on the top of the tank to the flame arrester. The flame arrester end of this pipe was threaded.

---

[10] Bethune Point WWTP Facility Upgrade project specifications prepared by CDM, under contract to the City of Daytona Beach, section 11354, Methanol Feed System.

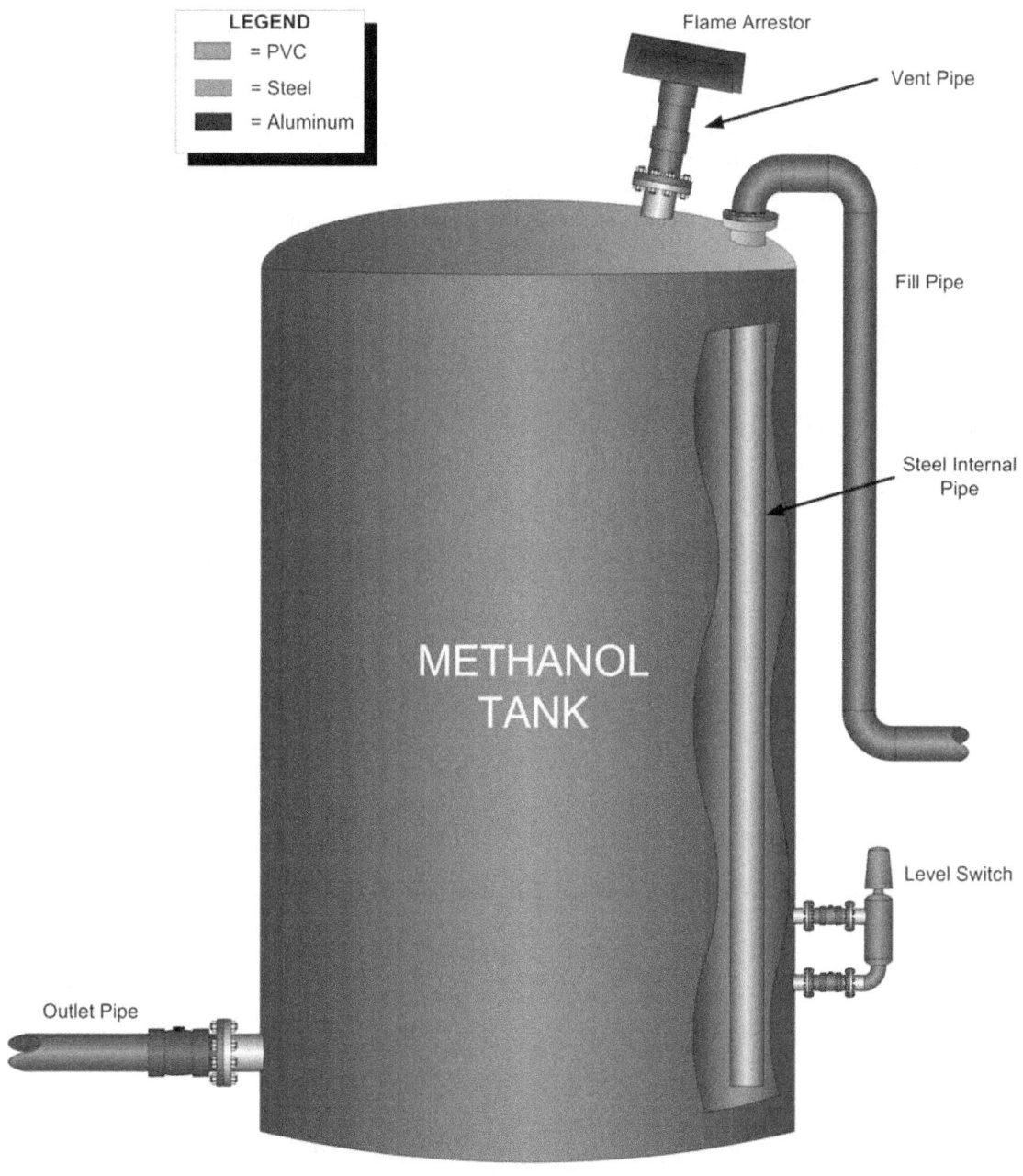

Figure 4. Aboveground PVC methanol pipes

3.3.2   Piping Specifications and Standards

The CDM methanol system specification[11] required that "[t]he entire system shall comply with all applicable OSHA rules and regulations." Therefore, OSHA standard 1910.106, "Flammable and Combustible Liquids," would have applied to this installation. This standard requires that all aboveground piping containing flammable liquids be steel, nodular iron, or malleable iron. The tensile strength and fracture toughness[12] of steel is more than ten times greater than the PVC plastic pipe used for the methanol system.

OSHA standard 1910.106 does allow materials that soften on fire exposure such as plastics, but only when "necessary." CDM stated[13] that it specified PVC for its compatibility with methanol and its ability to withstand the system pressure. The CSB noted that published corrosion data indicate that steel is compatible with methanol, that steel piping is widely used in flammable liquid systems, and that the methanol tank specified by CDM was made of steel. From this, the CSB concluded that no necessity to use PVC pipe existed.

The CDM methanol tank specification[14] required that the tank comply with National Fire Protection Association Standard (NFPA) 30, Flammable and Combustible Liquids Code (1990). NFPA 30 section 3-3.3 requires that all valves connected to storage tanks be steel. Despite this requirement, CDM

---

[11] Bethune Point WWTP Upgrade project specifications (idem).

[12] Fracture toughness is a measure of a materials ability to resist brittle failure.

[13] In response to an interrogatory in which the CSB asked CDM to describe the necessity for using PVC piping.

[14] Bethune WWTP Upgrade project specifications prepared by CDM, under contract to the City of Daytona Beach, section 13515, Methanol Chemical Storage Tank.

informed Indian River Industrial Contractor Inc. (IRIC), the facility constructor, that PVC ball valves could be used.[15]

Although NFPA 30 and OSHA standard 1910.106 permit plastic materials in aboveground flammable liquid systems under certain conditions, other widely recognized standards prohibit them. These include the American Society of Mechanical Engineers (ASME) Process Piping Code, ASME B31.3[16] and the Building Officials Code Administrators (BOCA) National Mechanical Code, Seventh Edition.[17]

3.3.3   Piping Failure

The physical evidence indicates that the PVC piping connected to the methanol tank mechanically failed in multiple locations from the upward movement of the tank caused by the internal explosion. This evidence includes:

- The burn pattern on the side of the tank, which most likely occurred when pressure from the internal explosion forced methanol up an internal pipe and sprayed it out of the separated fill pipe onto the side of the tank.

- The burn pattern on the ground east of the tank, which most likely occurred when pressure from the explosion sprayed methanol onto the ground through the failed outlet pipe connected near the bottom of the tank.

- Two PVC valves and a portion of the connected pipe found in the concrete containment that surrounded the tank. These valves and their associated PVC pipe and flanges were installed between

---

[15] CDM response to an IRIC request for information dated May 12, 1993.

[16] Chapter VII, Nonmetallic Piping and Piping Lined with Nonmetals, paragraph A323.4.2 (a) (1).

[17] Article 9, Flammable and Combustible Liquid Storage and Piping Systems, paragraph M-901.5.

steel flanges on the tank and steel flanges on the level switch. A recovered valve shows the fractured

PVC pipe between the valve and flange (Figure 5).

Figure 5. Failed 1-inch PVC pipe showing fracture surface

- PVC material lodged in the threads of the flame arrester and visible damage to the threads on the end
  of the PVC vent pipe.

The two fractured PVC pipes supporting the level switch pointed directly toward the crane cab where the

mechanic was sitting. Methanol discharging under pressure most likely sprayed the cab, ignited and

seriously burned the mechanic inside. Figure 6 shows the burned-out cab aligned with the 1-inch pipe

flanges on the tank.

Figure 6. Methanol spray from 1-inch pipe flanges onto the crane cab.

The PVC vent pipe was below the man-lift basket. After the flame arrester blew off the vent pipe, burning methanol vapors under pressure would have likely discharged into the basket where two workers were standing. Figure 7 shows the location of the basket relative to the vent pipe.

Figure 7. Location of man-lift basket and 4-inch vent pipe

Had the methanol piping and valves been constructed of steel, the system would most likely have remained intact. The mechanic in the crane would likely not have been killed, and the other two workers may have been less severely injured.

3.4   Methanol Tank Flame Arrester

The methanol storage tank vent was equipped with a flame arrester in accordance with NFPA 30. Flame arresters are devices that stop a flame while allowing gases and vapors to flow freely and work by channeling gas and/or vapor through narrow gaps between metal plates. The transfer of heat to the plates extinguishes a flame moving through the gaps. Proper sizing of the gaps and plates is critical to the flame arrester performance. Any blockage in the gaps or corrosion of the plates can render a flame arrester ineffective.

The flame arrester on the methanol storage tank vent pipe was a Protectoseal Model No. 864 (Figure 8). Because the vent through the flame arrester was always open, the tank discharged methanol vapors when filled or warmed and took in air when drained or cooled.

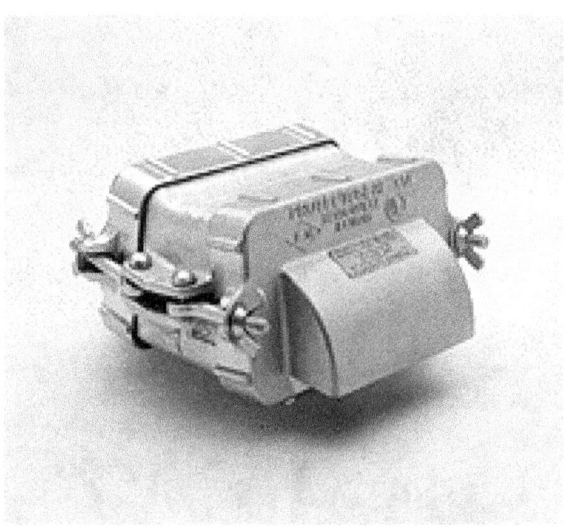

Figure 8. Protectoseal Model No. 864 flame arrester

(picture courtesy of Protectoseal)

The flame arrester plates and housing were aluminum. Published corrosion data[18] indicates that methanol corrodes aluminum. The flame arrester was severely corroded on the interior surface, the plates were clogged with aluminum oxide scale, and plates were broken with portions missing (Figure 9 and Figure 10). Corrosion on the broken plate edges indicates that the broken plate damage most likely occurred prior to the incident.

---

[18] NACE International, The Corrosion Society (2002). Corrosion Survey Database (COR·SUR). NACE International.

Figure 9. Flame arrester plate corrosion (outside)

Figure 10. Flame arrester plate corrosion (inside)

Correspondence among the construction company (IRIC); the construction manager (CDM); and the City of Daytona Beach indicated that the need for a flame arrester was identified late in the project. IRIC proposed three models for purchase, all of which had aluminum plates installed in an aluminum housing. CDM selected the Protectoseal Model 864 because it was readily available. Although Protectoseal offered flame arresters made of materials not corroded by methanol, none of these was proposed or selected.

Flame arresters require regular inspection and maintenance (cleaning) to maintain functionality. Dirt and small particles collecting in the narrow gaps between the flame arrester plates, insects nesting in the housing, and corrosion can degrade performance. Regular inspection can identify excessive corrosion. In 1993, when the methanol system became operational, both Protectoseal[19] and a major methanol producer[20] recommended regular flame arrester maintenance and inspection. However, no requirement for flame arrester maintenance and inspection was included with the operation and maintenance instructions CDM provided the City. Interviews indicate that Bethune Point WWTP personnel were unaware of the need to inspect and maintain the flame arrester.

The CSB concluded that the flame arrester did not prevent the fire outside the tank from igniting the tank contents. Routine inspections would have detected the corrosion in the flame arrester that occurred over 12 years. The use of an aluminum flame arrester in methanol service, coupled with the lack of inspection and maintenance, allowed the flame arrester to corrode to the point that it no longer functioned.

---

[19] From literature normally provided by Protectoseal with flame arresters.

[20] Based on a DuPont methanol product guide provided by CDM and found in the City of Daytona Beach contract file for the 1993 upgrades to the Bethune Point WWTP.

4.0   Regulatory Analysis

4.1   OSHA Regulations

The City of Daytona Beach was not required to comply with or implement OSHA regulations. Had the city implemented hot work and HAZCOM programs conforming to OSHA safety standards, the hazards of using a torch in proximity to the methanol tank would likely have been identified and possibly prevented.

Public employers are not covered by the Occupational Safety and Health Act of 1970 because section 3(5) of the act defines "employer" as "a person engaged in a business affecting commerce that has employees, but does not include the United States (not including the United States Postal Service) or any State or political subdivision of a State."

The Occupational Safety and Health Act includes two opportunities for city, county, and state employers to provide OSHA coverage: "state plans" and "public employee-only plans." Section 18 of the Act authorizes states to establish their own occupational safety and health programs, or "state plans," and Section 18(c)(6) requires all states that run their own state plans to establish "an effective and comprehensive occupational safety and health program applicable to all employees of public agencies of the State and its political subdivisions." Twenty one states have adopted OSHA state plans. OSHA regulation 29 CFR 1956.1 allows states that do not have state plans to adopt "public employee-only plans" to provide OSHA coverage even where no state plan covering private employers is in effect. Three states have adopted these "public employee plans" Appendix B includes a list of states and their OSHA coverage.

The federal government establishes staffing and enforcement benchmarks for "state plans" and "public employee-only plans" to ensure enforcement and standards are "at least as effective" as the federal program. The state programs must also adopt all OSHA standards or issue their own standards that are "at least as effective as" OSHA standards. The federal government matches funding for approved "state plans" and "public employee-only plans."[21]

OSHA coverage provides four major benefits to employees:

- Coverage by OSHA standards (or equivalent state standards). Most of these are in 29 CFR 1910 (General Industry) and 1926 (Construction).

- Ability to file a complaint and receive an OSHA inspection without fear of employer retaliation.

- Right to participate in, receive the results of OSHA inspections, and have an opening and closing conference with the OSHA inspector separate from the employer.

- Ability to request and receive information from the employer on workplace monitoring of chemicals, noise and radiation levels, and chemical hazards covered by the OSHA HAZCOM standard. The Occupational Safety and Health Act also gives employees the right to review their employer's injury and illness log and relevant exposure and medical records.

Some of the remaining 26 states without "state plans" and "public employee-only plans" provide safety and health protection to public employees, although these programs do not receive federal funding and are not subject to federal OSHA oversight. Florida had such a program until it was eliminated in 2000.

---

[21] Further information about state plans is available at http://www.osha.gov/dcsp/osp/index html.

31

4.2   Florida Public Employee Safety

4.2.1   History

The Florida Occupational Safety and Health Act,[22] enacted in 1982, directed the Florida Division of Safety (a division within the Department of Labor and Employment Security) to assist employers (both private and public, including cities and counties) to make their workplaces safer and decrease the frequency and severity of on-the-job injuries. State, city, and county employers were required to comply with most OSHA regulations and the state had the authority to cite public employers.

The Florida legislature repealed Chapter 442 in 1999.[23] Until its repeal, the Florida legislature appropriated approximately $11 million per year for occupational safety and health programs, which funded a statewide staff of 146 employees, 21 of whom worked in a consulting program for private small businesses that received matching funds from the federal government. The remaining 125 staff members addressed public sector (i.e., state and municipal employers) occupational safety and health compliance.

Following the repeal of Chapter 442, the governor issued an executive order[24] addressing public employee safety and health. State agencies listed in the executive order were directed "to voluntarily comply" with General Industry OSHA standards.[25] The executive order recommends that each city and county (as well as state agencies not specifically covered in the first part of the executive order) "review… existing policies, practices and procedures concerning workplace safety and implement any policies, practices or

---

[22] Florida Statutes, Chapter 442.20.

[23] Chapter 2001-65, House Bill No. 669. The repeal was effective July 1, 2000.

[24] Florida Executive Order Number 2000-292 dated September 25, 2000.

[25] 29 CFR 1910, Subparts C through T and Subpart Z. Construction standards in 29 CFR 1926 are excluded.

procedures made necessary by the repeal of Chapter 442."[26] The Florida legislature provided no funding to state agencies, cities or counties to implement the executive order.

Today, no Florida state laws or regulations exist to require municipalities to implement safe work practices for or communicate chemical hazards to municipal employees.

4.2.2   Florida Municipal Safety Program Survey

The CSB conducted a telephone survey of six Florida cities and three Florida counties to determine the extent of their voluntary compliance with OSHA standards. As part of the survey, the CSB investigators interviewed occupational safety and health or loss control managers.

Most entities surveyed reported having policies requiring compliance with OSHA standards. In some cases, the CSB also spoke with union representatives at the surveyed city or county. Some union representatives confirmed voluntary compliance with OSHA standards, but others described hazardous conditions and incidents indicating that OSHA standards and good safety practices are not fully implemented and that conditions are not evaluated or remedied, despite employee complaints.

Voluntary compliance with OSHA standards does not provide public sector employees with all the rights conveyed to private sector employees (and covered public sector employees) under the Occupational Safety and Health Act. Even if the employer conforms with all OSHA General Industry standards, employees remain without the legal right to receive an OSHA inspection or to review relevant records and medical and exposure information. Additionally, non-mandatory safety programs are vulnerable to changes in budgetary priorities.

_____

[26] Although mandatory for state agencies, other political subdivisions and the public have no legal obligation to comply with an executive order issued by the governor.

4.2.3 Florida Public Facility Chemical Incidents

In addition to surveying several Florida cities and counties, the CSB researched[27] the frequency and severity of chemical incidents at Florida public facilities. In addition to the incident at the Bethune WWTP, the CSB found 33 additional chemical incidents at public facilities in the last five years. The incidents resulted in 9 injuries, 23 medical evaluations for chemical exposure, and 15 evacuations involving the facility or surrounding community. All of these incidents involved chemicals that would normally be included in an OSHA compliant hazard communication program.

4.2.4 Safety Consultation

The University of South Florida administers a voluntary private sector worker safety consultation program for the State of Florida. Half of the program funding comes from the Florida's Workers' Compensation Trust Fund, the other half as matching funds from the U.S. Department of Labor.[28] The program has a state-wide staff of 17 and offers confidential health and safety compliance consulting to private small business owners, with the goal of encouraging them to voluntarily improve workplace safety. Because of restrictions on federal funding, the program is prohibited from offering consultation to Florida's public employers.

---

[27] Media reports, National Response Center reports and the EPA Risk Management Program database.

[28] Section 21(d) of the Occupational Safety and Health Act of 1970 authorizes states to enter into a cooperative agreement with OSHA and receive matching Federal funds for consultation programs.

5.0 Key Findings

1.   The City of Daytona Beach has no program, written or otherwise, to control hot work at city facilities.

2.   The CSB found no evidence that workers at the Bethune Point WWTP received any methanol hazard training in the last 10 years.

3.   The City of Daytona Beach does not require work plan reviews to evaluate the safety of non-routine tasks.

4.   OSHA 1910.106 permits the use of plastic piping in flammable liquid piping systems when necessary but does not define necessary.

5.   NFPA 30 permits the use of plastic piping in flammable liquid piping systems under certain conditions.

6.   The methanol tank did not comply with NFPA 30. Valves and their connection to the tank were PVC instead of steel.

7.   The failure of the PVC piping attached to the tank and in the methanol system greatly increased the consequences of the incident.

8.   Flame arrester maintenance requirements were not included in the operation and maintenance manual for the methanol system.

9.   An aluminum flame arrester was installed on the methanol tank; methanol corrodes aluminum.

10. The flame arrester was not inspected or cleaned since its installation in 1993.

11.   The flame arrester was so degraded (gaps between the plates inside the flame arrester were plugged with dirt and aluminum oxide and portions of the plates were corroded away) that it did not prevent a flame from entering the tank which greatly increased the consequences of the incident.

12.   No Florida state laws or regulations exist to require municipalities to implement safe work practices.

13.   No Florida state laws or regulations exist to require municipalities to communicate chemical hazards to municipal employees.

14.   Florida municipalities are not covered by OSHA workplace safety standards.

15.   No state or federal oversight of public employee safety exists in the State of Florida.

6.0 Root and Contributing Causes

6.1 Root Causes

The City of Daytona Beach

1.   did not implement adequate controls for hot work at the Bethune Point WWTP; and

2.   had an ineffective HAZCOM program.

6.2 Contributing Causes

1.   The City of Daytona Beach has no systematic program to evaluate the safety of non-routine tasks.

2.   The aboveground piping and valves in the methanol system were constructed of PVC in lieu of steel.

3.   An aluminum flame arrester was installed on the methanol tank even though methanol is known to corrode aluminum.

4.   The operation and maintenance manual for the Bethune Point WWTP did not include a requirement to maintain the flame arrester.

7.0 Recommendations

The CSB makes recommendations based on the findings and conclusions of the investigation. Recommendations are made to parties that can affect change to prevent future incidents, which may include the facility where the incident occurred, the parent company, industry organizations responsible for developing good practice guidelines, regulatory bodies, and/or organizations that have the ability to broadly communicate lessons learned from the incident, such as trade associations and labor unions.

Governor and Legislature of the State of Florida

2006-03-I-FL-R1

Enact legislation requiring state agencies and each political subdivision (i.e. counties and municipalities) of Florida to implement policies, practices, procedures, including chemical hazards covering the workplace health and safety of Florida public employees that are at least as effective as OSHA. Establish and fund a mechanism to ensure compliance with these standards.

Consider legislation providing coverage of Florida public employees under an occupational safety and health program in accordance with Section 18(b) of the Occupational Safety and Health Act of 1970, and Code of Federal Regulations 29 CFR 1956.1.

2006-03-I-FL-R2

Develop and fund a workplace safety and health consultation program for Florida public employees similar to the private sector program currently administered by the Florida Safety Consultation Program at the University of South Florida.

City of Daytona Beach

2006-03-I-FL-R3

Adopt city ordinances to require departments to implement policies, practices, and procedures concerning safety and health in the workplace for city employees that are at least as effective as relevant OSHA standards. Emphasize compliance with chemical standards, including hot work procedures (OSHA Welding, Cutting, and Brazing Standard, Sections 1910.251 and 1910.252) and chemical hazard communication (OSHA Hazard Communication Standard 29 CFR 1910.1200). Implement procedures to ensure compliance with these policies, practices and procedures.

2006-03-I-FL-R4

Ensure that flammable liquid storage tanks used throughout the city comply with NFPA 30 and minimum federal standards in 29 CFR 1910.106, including appropriate piping and flame arresters.

National Fire Protection Association

2006-03-I-FL-R5

Revise NFPA 30 to specifically exclude the use of thermoplastics in aboveground flammable liquid service.

U.S. Department of Labor, Occupational Safety and Health Administration

2006-03-I-FL-R6

Revise 29 CFR 1910.106 to specifically exclude the use of thermoplastics in aboveground flammable liquid service.

Water Environment Federation

2006-03-I-FL-R7

Work with the Methanol Institute to prepare and distribute a technical bulletin containing information on the safe receipt, storage, use, and dispensing of methanol in wastewater treatment plants. In addition, include information on basic fire and explosion prevention measures when using bulk methanol (e.g., flame arrester maintenance, hot work programs, electrical classification).

2006-03-I-FL-R8

Work with the Methanol Institute to prepare safety training materials for wastewater treatment facilities that use methanol.

Methanol Institute

2006-03-I-FL-R9

Work with the Water Environment Federation to prepare and distribute a technical bulletin containing information on the safe receipt, storage, use, and dispensing of methanol in wastewater treatment plants. In addition, include information on basic fire and explosion prevention measures when using bulk methanol (e.g., flame arrester maintenance, hot work programs, electrical classification).

2006-03-I-FL-R10

Work with the Water Environment Federation to prepare safety training materials for wastewater treatment facilities that use methanol.

Camp Dresser & McKee Inc.

2006-03-I-FL-R11

Revise CDM policies and procedures to ensure that appropriate quality control measures are applied so that designs specify appropriate materials and comply with applicable safety standards. Ensure that wastewater treatment plant design engineers are aware of the importance of proper material selection as well as the findings and recommendations of this report.

2006-03-I-FL-R12

Communicate the findings and recommendations of this report to all companies that contracted with CDM for methanol and other flammable liquid systems that were constructed with aboveground plastic pipe. Recommend replacing plastic pipe with an appropriate material in accordance with NFPA 30 and OSHA 1910.106.

2006-03-I-FL-R13

Communicate the findings and recommendations of this report to all companies that contracted with CDM for flammable liquid systems that included a flame arrester. Emphasize the importance of periodic maintenance of the flame arrester to ensure its effective performance.

By the

U.S. Chemical Safety and Hazard Investigation Board

Carolyn W. Merritt
Chair

John S. Bresland
Member

Gary Visscher
Member

William Wark
Member

William Wright
Member

Date of Board Approval

8.0 References

American Society of Mechanical Engineers (ASME), 1999, *Process Piping Code*, ASME B31.3.

Center for Chemical Process Safety (CCPS), 1995. *Guidelines for Safe Process Operations and Maintenance,* American Institute of Chemical Engineers (AIChE).

Florida, 2006a. *Fire Prevention and Control* Florida Statutes, Chapter 663.

Florida, 2006b. *The Florida Fire Prevention Code,* Florida Administrative Code, Chapter 69A-60.

Lees, F. P., 2001. *Loss Prevention in the Process Industries*, Vol. 3, Butterworth-Heinemann.

National Fire Protection Association (NFPA), 2003a. *Fire protection in Wastewater Treatment Plants*, NFPA 820.

NFPA, 2003b. *Standard for Fire Prevention During Welding, Cutting and other Hot Work*, NFPA 51B.

NFPA, 2003c. *Uniform Fire Code*, NFPA 1.

NFPA, 2003d. *Uniform Fire Code-Florida Edition*, NFPA 1.

Occupational Safety and Health Administration (OSHA), 2006. *Flammable and combustible liquids*, 29 CFR 1910.106, OSHA.

Pegula, S. M., 2004. *Fatal Occupational Injuries to Government Workers, 1992 to 2001*, Bureau of Labor Statistics, 2004.

Appendix A: ROOT CAUSE LOGIC DIAGRAM

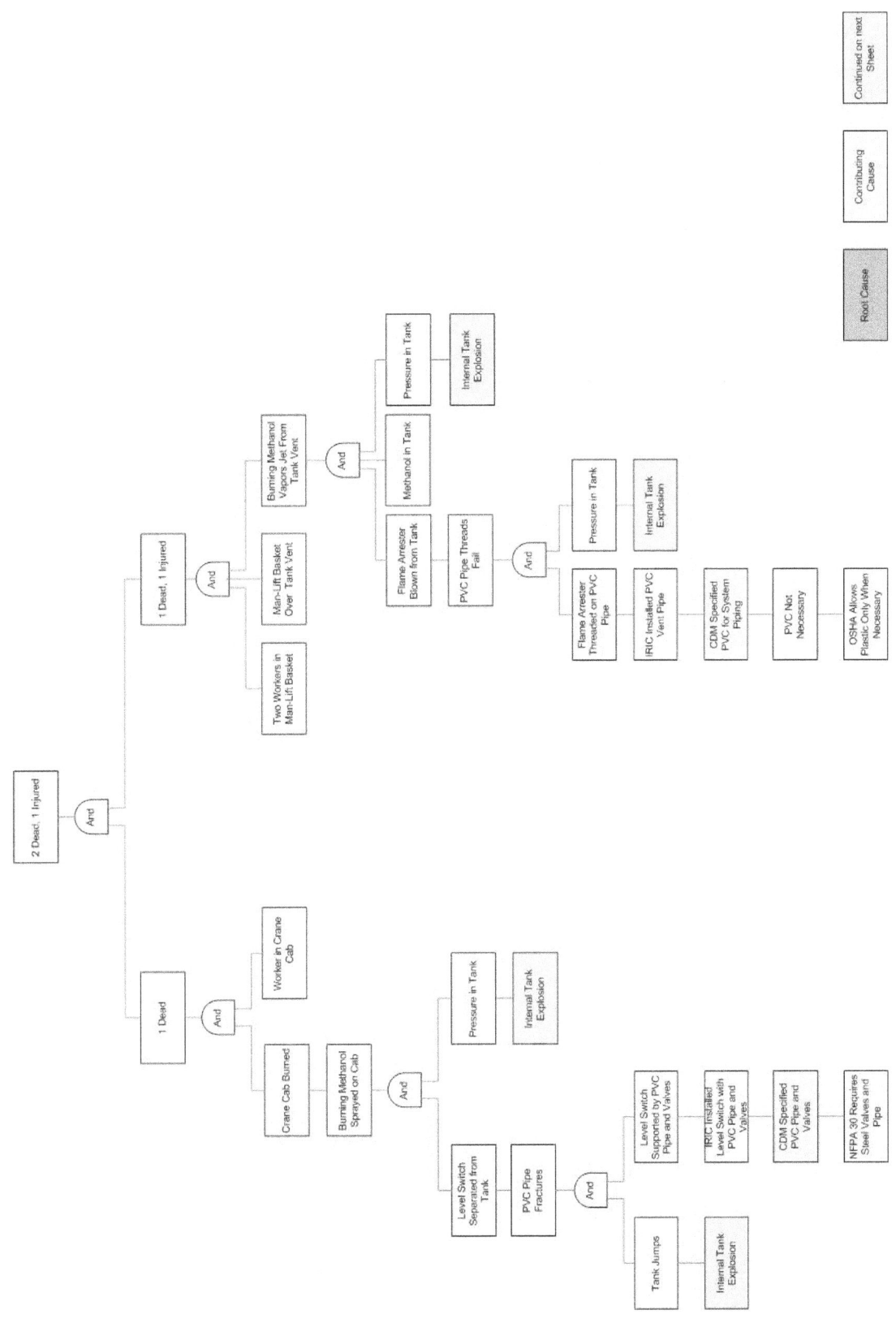

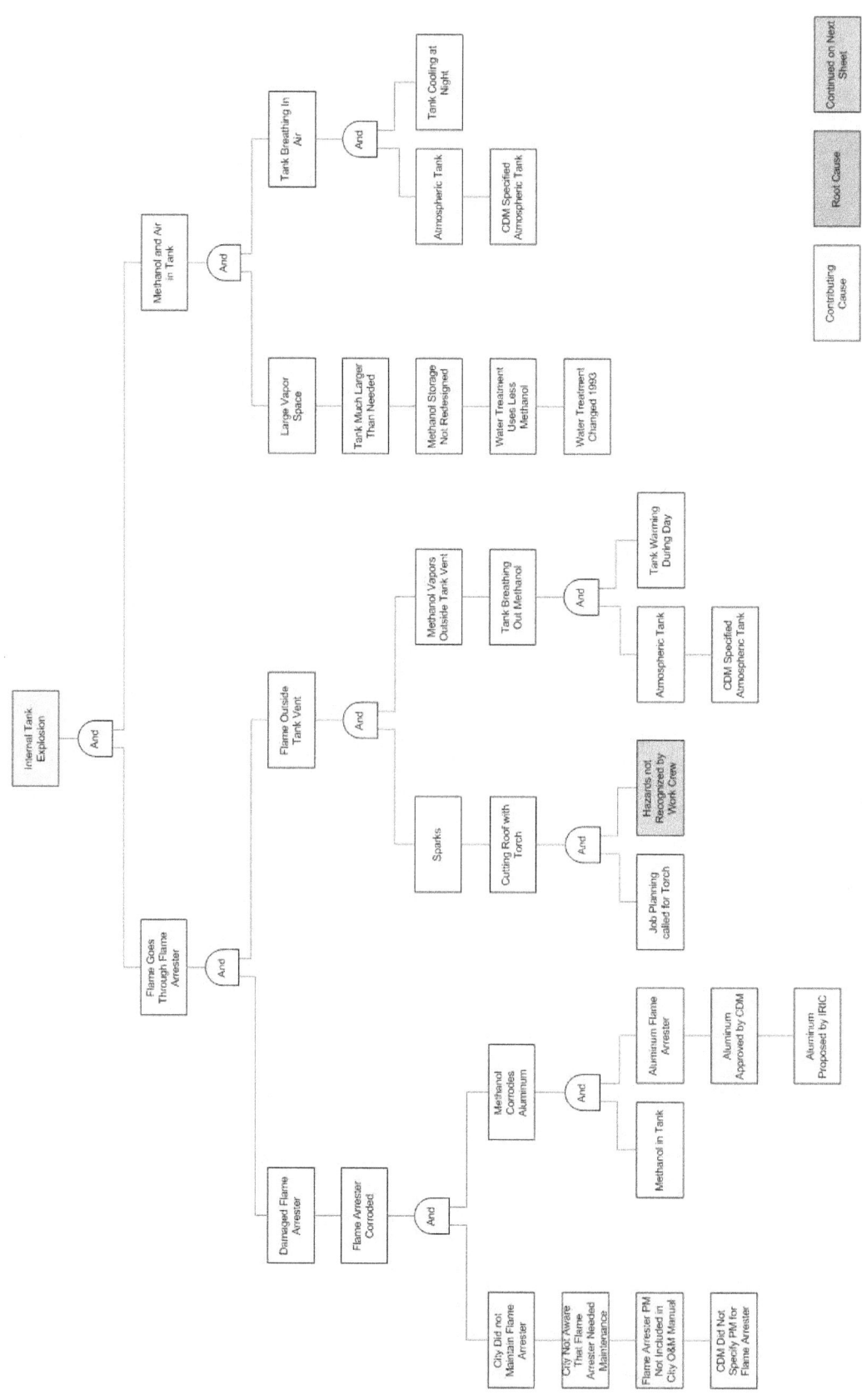

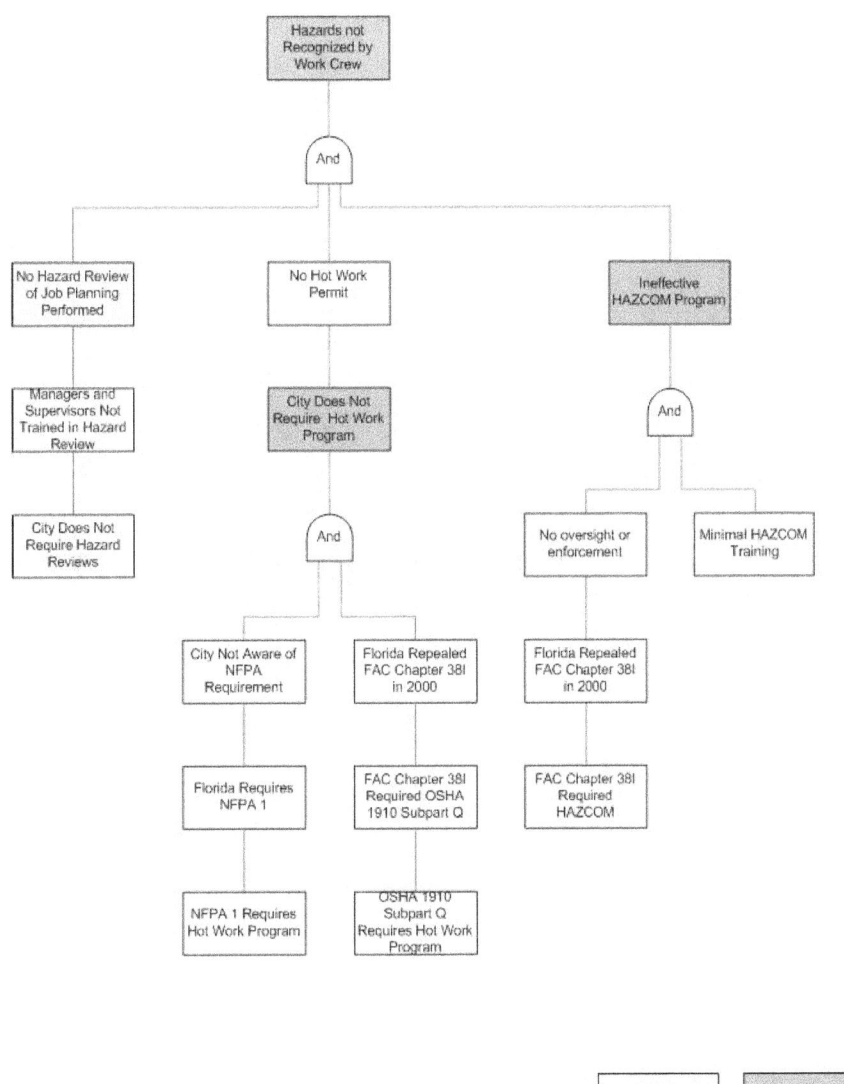

Appendix B: PUBLIC EMPLOYEE OSHA COVERAGE

PUBLIC EMPLOYEE OSHA COVERAGE

State	OSHA Coverage
Alabama	
Alaska	State Plan
Arizona	State Plan
Arkansas	
California	State Plan
Colorado	
Connecticut	Public Employee Only Plan
Delaware	
Florida	
Georgia	
Hawaii	State Plan
Illinois	
Indiana	State Plan
Iowa	State Plan
Kansas	
Kentucky	State Plan
Louisiana	
Maine	
Maryland	State Plan
Massachusetts	
Michigan	State Plan
Minnesota	State Plan
Mississippi	
Missouri	
Montana	
Nebraska	
Nevada	State Plan
New Hampshire	
New Jersey	Public Employee Only Plan
New Mexico	State Plan

State	OSHA Coverage
New York	Public Employee Only Plan
North Carolina	State Plan
North Dakota	
Ohio	
Oklahoma	
Oregon	State Plan
Pennsylvania	
Puerto Rico	State Plan
Rhode Island	
South Carolina	State Plan
Tennessee	State Plan
Texas	
Utah	State Plan
Vermont	State Plan
Virgin Islands	Public Employee Only Plan
Virginia	State Plan
Washington	State Plan
West Virginia	
Wisconsin	
Wyoming	State Plan

www.ingramcontent.com/pod-product-compliance
Lightning Source LLC
Chambersburg PA
CBHW081623170526
45166CB00009B/3076